THE HIGH PROTEIN COOK
LOUISE KANG
HIGH PROTEIN
CLASSICS
20 EASY HIGH PROTEIN VERSIONS OF YOUR FAVOURITE MEALS

CONTENTS

HELLO

and welcome to my first cookbook ☺

Inside you will find 20 of my most popular High Protein creations, all of which have over 20g of protein per serving.

This book is completely interactive – every recipe has an instruction video to go with it which you can click through to from the eBook. To download the eBook free of charge, head to http://classics.highproteincook.com

I'd love to find out how you get on with these recipes. I create several new ones every week so be sure to follow me on social media.

Louise

Louise

Website: http://highproteincook.com

Facebook: http://facebook.com/highproteincook

Instagram: http://instagram.com/highproteincook

Snapchat: http://snapchat.com/add/highproteincook

HEALTHIER
SWEET & SOUR CHICKEN

SERVES 2

15 MINS PREP
15 MINS COOK

INGREDIENTS

1 chicken breast, chopped into
bite-sized cubes

½ a beaten egg

1 tablespoon cornflour

1 yellow pepper, sliced
lengthwise into long strips

½ a large onion, finely sliced

1 red chilli pepper, deseeded and
sliced lengthwise into long strips

1 clove of garlic, chopped

4½oz/130g fresh or canned pineapple

3 teaspoons oil

1 tablespoon toasted sesame seeds
(optional)

salt & pepper

FOR THE SAUCE

2½oz/75ml pineapple juice

1 tablespoon cornflour

1 tablespoon tomato ketchup

1 tablespoon soy sauce

1 tablespoon white wine vinegar

1 teaspoon honey

METHOD

1. Place the chicken breast cubes into a small bowl containing the beaten egg, cornflour and a good sprinkling of salt and pepper. Mix well so that the chicken cubes are completely coated. Keep this bowl aside.

2. To prepare the sauce: place the cornflour in a cup and add a tablespoon or two of the pineapple juice. Mix well with a spoon until the cornflour has completely dissolved (this step is to avoid lumps). Now add the rest of the pineapple juice as well as the other sauce ingredients, mixing well.

3. Heat up 1 teaspoon of the oil in a frying pan on medium heat. Add the sliced onion, yellow pepper and red chilli pepper and keep stirring for around 3 - 4 minutes, until the onion starts becoming translucent. At this point, add the garlic and cook for another minute or two, until the onion has lost its crunch and the garlic has browned a little.

4. Remove the vegetables from the pan into a bowl and set aside. Return the pan to the stove and heat the remaining oil. Once the oil is hot, add the chicken cubes.

5. Spread the chicken cubes around the pan so that they are all touching the bottom. After around 3 minutes, check to see if the underside of the chicken is cooked and, if so, flip them over to cook the other side.

6. After another 3 minutes, or when the other side of the chicken cubes is cooked, stir the chicken around for a minute or so and then add in the cooked vegetables and sauce.

7. Turn the heat down and stir for a few minutes, until everything becomes coated in the sticky sauce. The sauce should thicken during this time.

8. Right before serving, add the pineapple pieces and stir for another minute so that they warm up a little.

421 CALORIES   30g PROTEIN   14g FAT   45g CARBS

MACROS (PER PORTION, EXCLUDING RICE)

Recipe notes:
• This recipe really does only need
half a beaten egg (or you could
use a yolk or a white). Use the
other half to make scrambled eggs
or an omelette.

SUPER HIGH PROTEIN
BUTTER CHICKEN

SERVES 4

10 MINS PREP
15 MINS COOK

INGREDIENTS

4 chicken breasts,
   cut into bite-sized pieces

1 teaspoon cumin

2 tablespoons ground fenugreek

2 heaped teaspoons Greek yoghurt
   (regular is best rather than fat-free)

2 tablespoons tomato puree

3 tablespoons/45g butter

3 cloves

3 cardamom pods, crushed

1 cinnamon stick,
   broken into two pieces

1 green chilli pepper, finely chopped

1 tablespoon ginger (a thumb-sized
   piece), finely chopped

3 garlic cloves, chopped

1 cup/250g passata (sieved tomatoes)

1 tablespoon smooth peanut butter

1 teaspoon sugar or sweetener

½ teaspoon garam masala (optional)

METHOD

1. Season the chicken breast pieces with salt and pepper. Add the cumin, 1 tablespoon of ground fenugreek, the tomato puree and 1 tablespoon of Greek yoghurt. Mix well, so the chicken pieces become completely covered, and keep aside.

2. Heat up the butter in a large saucepan on medium heat. When it has melted, add the cloves, cardamom and cinnamon stick and cook for 1 minute to flavour the butter. Then, add the chilli, garlic and ginger and cook for a minute longer, until the garlic has just started to become brown.

3. Add the yoghurt-covered chicken and cover the pan with a lid. Cook for 5 minutes, stirring once.

4. Lift the lid, add the passata and remaining ground fenugreek. Cook again, covered, for another 5 minutes, stirring once.

5. Turn off the heat and stir in the remaining Greek yoghurt, the peanut butter, garam masala (optional) and sugar or sweetener. Check the seasoning before serving and add more salt if needed.

> **Recipe notes:**
> • The most important ingredient in this recipe is the fenugreek, so don't be tempted to leave it out. I managed to find some in a larger supermarket.
> • The peanut butter may not be very authentic, but it works! The traditional recipe includes cream, which I first tried replacing with cashew butter, which is more expensive and doesn't work quite as well.

410 CALORIES 52g PROTEIN 14g FAT 16g CARBS

MACROS (PER PORTION)

THAI SWEET POTATO
FISHCAKES

SERVES 1-2

15 MINS PREP
15 MINS COOK

INGREDIENTS

1 medium sized sweet potato
(approx. weight 5^1/$_3$oz/150g)

1 tin of tuna, drained

1 spring onion, chopped

2 cloves of garlic, chopped

a handful of coriander, chopped

½ teaspoon fish sauce

1 teaspoon oil

METHOD

1. Peel the sweet potato and cut it into small
cubes. Place into a microwave-safe bowl and
microwave for 3 – 5 minutes, until the sweet potato
is fork tender.

2. Combine all of the ingredients in a large bowl and
mix well together. Leave the bowl in the fridge for
at least 30 minutes – this will help the mixture to firm
up a little. If you are short of time, you can skip this
step and instead beat in an egg to the mixture.

3. Heat up the oil in a large frying pan. Divide
the sweet potato mixture into small balls and place
each one into the pan. While they are frying, flatten
the balls with a spatula until they are around an
inch thin.

4. Once the first side has browned, carefully flip
over the fishcakes and fry the other side for another
few minutes.

5. Remove from the pan and serve.

Recipe notes:
• You can also use cooked salmon in place of tuna
for this recipe.
• If the mixture is too wet, add a little flour or
protein powder.

 340 CALORIES
 35g PROTEIN
6g FAT
 35g CARBS

MACROS (FOR THE ENTIRE BATCH)

CHICKEN JAMBALAYA

SERVES 5

15 MINS PREP
40-50 MINS COOK

INGREDIENTS

1 medium sized onion, chopped

2 peppers, deseeded and chopped

2 cloves of garlic, chopped finely

2 teaspoons oil

2 chicken breasts,
  cut into bite-sized cubes

3 – 4 teaspoons Cajun spice

1 teaspoon chilli powder

14oz/400g can chopped tomatoes

1½ cups/300g brown rice

14oz/400g can sweetcorn

1 chicken stock cube, dissolved
  in 2¾ cups/700g water

METHOD

1. Heat up 1 teaspoonful of the oil in a large pan and fry the onion. Once it has begun to get translucent, add the peppers and garlic.

2. After the vegetables have softened, remove from the pan. Add the remaining oil, add the chicken cubes to the pan and cook for a few minutes on medium heat until one side has become brown. Then, flip the chicken cubes and cook on the other side.

3. Once the chicken has browned evenly on both sides, add the vegetables back to the pan and add the Cajun spices, chilli powder and a little salt and pepper. Stir and cook for a few minutes.

4. Add the chopped tomatoes, rice, sweetcorn and stock.

5. Simmer on medium to low heat until the rice has cooked (check the packet for an indication of how long this will take) and the majority of the liquid has been absorbed. This should take about 30 – 40 minutes.

6. Serve hot, with a dollop of Greek yoghurt for extra protein.

Recipe notes:
- *You can make this into a true one-pan dish by cooking the chicken first until browned, and then adding the onions afterwards (followed by the peppers and garlic). However, I prefer to cook the onions separately as cooking them well will add a lot more flavour to the finished dish.*

416 CALORIES

27g PROTEIN

10g FAT
52g CARBS

MACROS
(INCLUDING RICE BUT EXCLUDING GREEK YOGHURT)

COURGETTI CARBONARA

SERVES 2

10 MINS PREP
15 MINS COOK

INGREDIENTS

10½oz/300g courgetti
(spiralized courgette)

½ cup/50g Parmesan cheese, grated

2 large egg yolks

1 clove of garlic (crushed and peeled)

black pepper

2oz/50g turkey bacon

METHOD

1. Dry-fry the turkey bacon in a non-stick frying pan (no need for oil) for about 5 minutes. When it is cooked, turn off the heat and allow it to cool a little. Cut the bacon into small strips using some kitchen scissors.

2. Separately, put almost all of the Parmesan cheese into a saucepan (keeping aside a handful to sprinkle over the top at the end) and add in the egg yolks, a good sprinkling of black pepper and the crushed garlic.

3. Whisk everything together, add the courgetti and stir well so that it becomes completely coated.

4. Put the heat on the lowest setting and let the courgetti begin to sweat. Once it has given out quite a bit of water, turn the heat up a little to thicken up the sauce.

5. When the sauce has become thick and smooth, turn off the heat. Add the chopped turkey bacon to the sauce and stir once to mix it properly with the sauce.

6. Serve with the remainder of the cheese sprinkled on top.

Recipe notes:
• If you can't find turkey bacon, use regular bacon for this dish (it will taste even better!).

 218 CALORIES 20g PROTEIN 13g FAT 6g CARBS

MACROS (PER SERVING)

FLUFFY COCONUT
PROTEIN PANCAKES

SERVES 1-2

5 MINS PREP
5 MINS COOK

INGREDIENTS

1 large egg

2 tablespoons coconut flour

¼ cup/25g scoop vanilla whey protein powder

¼ cup/50g Greek yoghurt

½ teaspoon baking powder

1 teaspoon oil (for frying)

METHOD

1. Break the egg into a mixing bowl and add the rest of the ingredients (except for the oil). Beat together with a fork or an egg-whisk until there are no lumps.

2. Heat up the oil in a frying pan and, once hot, spoon in the pancake batter (this quantity will make 4 pancakes, each of which uses 2 tablespoons of batter).

3. After a minute or two, flip the pancakes over with a spatula.

4. Cook the second side for around 30 seconds – 1 minute and then serve.

Recipe notes:
- *This recipe can be adapted to include any flavour of dairy or plant based protein powder.*
- *For extra-fluffy pancakes, whisk the egg using an electric mixer or blender before adding the other ingredients.*

 295 CALORIES
 36g PROTEIN
 14g FAT
 11g CARBS

MACROS (FOR THE ENTIRE BATCH)

CAULIFLOWER PIZZA

MAKES 1 PIZZA

10 MINS PREP
30 MINS COOK

INGREDIENTS

1½ cups/150g cauliflower rice
(see Recipe notes)

2 egg whites (= 4 tablespoon liquid
egg whites)

½ cup/50g mozzarella cheese

1 tablespoon coconut flour

your choice of toppings

METHOD

1. Preheat the oven to 180°C/350°F and line a pizza stone or baking tray with greaseproof paper.

2. Combine the cauliflower rice with the egg whites, mozzarella and 1 tablespoon of the coconut flour. Add a good grinding of salt & pepper and mix well.

3. Pour out the cauliflower mixture on top of the greaseproof paper, flattening it and giving it a pizza shape with your hands.

4. Bake the pizza base for around 10 minutes in the preheated oven.

5. Top with whatever you fancy and put it back into the oven for another 20 minutes.

Recipe notes:
- *Making cauliflower pizza used to be a long, messy process as you had to blast half of a cauliflower head in the food processor to make it into rice or couscous (or whatever you want to call it). However, now you can buy ready-blasted cauliflower in almost every supermarket.*

 230 CALORIES **22g** PROTEIN **11g** FAT **10g** CARBS

MACROS (BASE ONLY)

CHILLI CON CARNE

SERVES 4

10 MINS PREP
40 MINS COOK

INGREDIENTS

1 pound/500g lean mince

1 large onion, peeled and chopped

3 cloves of garlic, peeled and chopped

1 red pepper, deseeded and chopped

1 teaspoon chilli powder

1 teaspoon paprika

1 teaspoon cumin

1 cinnamon stick

1 tablespoon oil

1 beef stock cube

14oz/400g can of chopped tomatoes

14oz/400g can of red kidney beans

1 splash of Worcestershire sauce

1 piece of dark chocolate (optional)

1¼ cups/300ml water

METHOD

1. Heat up the oil in a large pan and fry the onion for a few minutes. Once the onion has started to soften and become translucent, add the garlic and red pepper. Stir for 1 – 2 minutes then add the chilli powder, cumin, paprika and add the cinnamon stick. Give everything a good stir and leave it to cook for around 3 – 5 minutes.

2. Add the mince to the pan and separate it with a fork, making sure it all gets a chance to brown. Keep the heat high while stirring regularly so that the mince fries rather than boils in its own juices.

3. Once the mince has evenly browned, add the can of tinned tomatoes, crumble in the beef stock cube and add the water. Turn down the heat and leave the pan to simmer for around 20 minutes. Stir occasionally to make sure that it doesn't burn.

4. Once the mixture is looking thick and juicy, add the red kidney beans and chocolate. Check the seasoning, stir well and leave for another few minutes.

5. Leave to sit for a few minutes and then serve with rice and a dollop of Greek yoghurt

Recipe notes:
* *Of course, the dark chocolate is optional. But if you choose to leave it out, the finished dish would really benefit from a pinch of sugar or sweetener.*

 300 CALORIES 33g PROTEIN 10g FAT 19g CARBS

MACROS
(PER SERVING, EXCLUDING RICE AND GREEK YOGHURT)

EASY PAD THAI

SERVES 2

15 MINS PREP
15 MINS COOK

INGREDIENTS

1 chicken breast, sliced very thinly
lengthwise with a sharp knife

1 large egg

3 spring onions, sliced very thinly
lengthwise

2 medium sized carrots, sliced very
thinly lengthwise

½ a large shallot (or 1 small one),
sliced thinly

20g peanuts (= approx. 20 nuts)

3½oz/100g rice noodles, soaked in
boiling water until softened

1 teaspoon of oil

1 tablespoon tamarind paste

1 tablespoon sweet chilli sauce

1 teaspoon fish sauce

1 teaspoon sugar or sweetener

a large handful of beansprouts

half a lime, sliced (to serve)

METHOD

1. Prepare the Pad Thai sauce: mix together the
tamarind paste, sweet chilli sauce, fish sauce and
sugar/sweetener with 2 tablespoons of water.

2. Separately, heat up the wok to a medium heat
and add the peanuts. Stir until the nuts are browned
(take care not to burn them!), then transfer to a
chopping board and chop. Put them aside
for serving.

3. Put the wok back on the stove, turn the heat up
to the maximum level and add the oil. Make sure
you have all of your ingredients ready, including the
noodles, which should be softened and drained,
before starting to stir-fry.

4. First, add the shallot and chicken and stir-fry for
1 – 2 minutes (until the chicken is no longer pink).
Move the chicken and shallot to the edge of the wok.

5. Break the egg into the centre of the wok and
stir continuously until it is scrambled (this should only
take seconds). Mix together with the chicken and
shallot.

6. Add the noodles, spring onions, carrots,
half of the beansprouts and Pad Thai sauce to this
mixture and cook for a few minutes, stirring
continuously.

7. Turn off the heat and serve with the chopped
peanuts and slices of lime.

MACROS (PER PORTION)

FAJITAS
WITH HOMEMADE GUACAMOLE

SERVES 2

15 MINS PREP
10 MINS COOK

INGREDIENTS

For the fajitas:
½ pound/200g lean steak, cut into strips (sirloin, skirt/flank or rump with most of the fat removed)
½ teaspoon cayenne pepper
½ teaspoon paprika
a pinch of cumin
½ teaspoon cornflour
2 teaspoon oil (any kind)
2 peppers (any colour), chopped lengthwise
1 onion, chopped lengthwise

For the guacamole:
1 ripe avocado
1 small ripe tomato
¼ of a red onion, chopped
¼ of a red chilli pepper, chopped
a handful of coriander leaves, chopped
juice of ½ a lime
salt & pepper

To serve
2 'light' tortilla wraps

hot sauce

METHOD

1. Add the cayenne pepper, paprika, cumin, cornflour and a good sprinkling of salt and pepper to the steak strips and mix together so that the strips are well coated.

2. Let the steak strips stay out of the fridge while you prepare the guacamole so that they reach room temperature.

3. For the guacamole, chop up the avocado, tomato, onion, chilli and coriander and mix together with the lime juice and a good grinding of salt and pepper.

4. Heat up 1 teaspoon of oil in a large frying pan or wok. Add the chopped onion and pepper. Cook them on high heat for a few minutes, until the onion becomes soft and loses its crunch.

5. Remove the onion and peppers from the pan, add the remaining oil and let it heat up until as hot as possible.

6. Add in the steak strips, making sure not to overcrowd the pan (cook them in 2 batches if necessary) and leave for approximately 1-2 minutes (until the outside is browned). Flip them over and cook for about 1 minute on the other side.

7. Remove the steak strips from the pan. Serve immediately with the tortilla wraps and guacamole.

> *Recipe notes:*
> * *Don't be put off by the long list of ingredients of this recipe. Of course, you can buy ready-made guacamole. But it's very easy and fairly quick to make your own.*
> * *The secret to cooking the steak strips well is getting your pan frighteningly hot. Don't forget that steak is at it's best when served rare or medium rather than well-done, so you only really need to brown the outside of the strips. If you cook the steak for too long, it will end up chewy.*

484 CALORIES 28g PROTEIN 23g FAT 40g CARBS

MACROS (PER SERVING, INCLUDING THE GUACAMOLE AND WRAP)

EASY
FISH PIE

SERVES 6

30 MINS PREP
55 MINS COOK

INGREDIENTS

3 large potatoes (weighing
approximately 2¼ pounds/1kg in total)

1 medium sized carrot, grated

2 sticks of celery, grated

1 red chilli, deseeded and chopped

1 lemon

1½ cups/150g strong cheddar, grated

25oz/700g of any fish (a mix of smoked
and unsmoked)

3 tablespoons olive oil

salt and pepper

METHOD

1. Peel and chop up the potatoes into small evenly sized pieces. Boil them in a saucepan of salted water for 10 minutes, or until soft. After they are done, remove them from the water and leave to sit in a colander for a few minutes so that they dry out a bit. Once you've done this, mash them with a fork and mix them with some salt, pepper and the olive oil.

2. Preheat your oven to 180°C/350°F. Add the carrot, celery, chilli and 1 cup/100g of the cheese into a large casserole dish.

3. Chop up the fish into bite sized pieces and remove any skin. Add this to the casserole dish, squeeze the juice out of the lemon over everything and mix all of the ingredients together, making sure they are well combined.

4. Top with the mashed potatoes and the remaining cheese. Bake the casserole dish in the preheated oven for around 45 minutes before serving.

Recipe notes:
- *Both white and sweet potatoes work really well in this recipe.*
- *Don't be tempted to leave out the lemon: it really transforms the dish. And even if you aren't a big fan of raw celery, give it a try as it really comes into its own when cooked.*

500 CALORIES   33g PROTEIN   23g FAT   39g CARBS

MACROS (PER SERVING)

MEATZA

SERVES 2

15 MINS PREP
20 MINS COOK

INGREDIENTS

1 pound/500g ground turkey

1 tablespoon tomato ketchup

1 red pepper, deseeded and chopped

½ a medium sized red onion,
peeled and chopped

2 cloves of garlic, finely chopped

a handful of spinach leaves

2½oz/70g cheese, sliced

3 tablespoons tomato puree

2 teaspoons oil

salt & pepper

METHOD

1. First cook the vegetables: heat 1 teaspoon of the oil in a frying pan until medium hot. Then, fry the onion and garlic in this oil for 1 minute. Add the rest of the vegetables to the pan and cook for a further 5 minutes, until they start to soften.

2. Remove the vegetables from the pan and add the rest of the oil. While it is heating up, season the mince with salt and pepper and add the tomato ketchup. Mix everything together well.

3. When the oil is hot, add all of the mince and flatten with a fork so that the whole base of the frying pan is covered.

4. After the first side of the mince base has browned (this should take around 5 minutes - you will be able to tell by looking at the edges), carefully flip it over.

5. Cover the mince base with the tomato puree, add a little more seasoning and then add the cooked vegetables and cheese.

6. Place a lid over the pan so that the whole mixture cooks evenly (and the cheese melts).

7. After 5 minutes, turn off the heat and carefully cut the cooked Meatza up into half.

> *Recipe notes:*
> * *This recipe also works really well using very lean steak mince.*
> * *Flipping over the Meatza (step 4) can be tricky – the best way is to turn off the heat and place a plate over the Meatza base. Place the palm of one of your hands over the plate and, using the other hand, flip the pan over.*

 480 CALORIES
 66g PROTEIN
 18g FAT
 13g CARBS

MACROS (PER SERVING)

PALAK PANEER
(SPINACH & PANEER CHEESE CURRY)

SERVES 2

10 MINS PREP
15 MINS COOK

INGREDIENTS

½ pound/300g bag of fresh baby
    spinach, rinsed and drained

a few sprays of cooking oil

½ large onion, peeled and sliced thinly

3 cloves of garlic, peeled and
    sliced thinly

1 tablespoon grated ginger

2 heaped tablespoons/100g jalfrezi paste

2 ripe tomatoes, chopped
    (or use tinned chopped tomatoes)

1 heaped tablespoon of Greek yoghurt

3 ½oz/100g paneer cheese
    (cut into cubes)

METHOD

1. Heat up a large frying pan or non-stick wok and add a few sprays of oil. Keeping the temperature low, add in the onion and fry for a few minutes, stirring often and adding a little water if necessary so that it doesn't burn.

2. Add the garlic, grated ginger and stir in the jalfrezi paste. Fry for a few minutes, stirring often, before adding the tomatoes. Let the mixture simmer for 2 – 3 minutes, until the onion has completely lost its crunch.

3. Add the spinach and carefully fold it in to the onion mixture (you will probably have to add it in batches unless you have a huge pan). Cook it on low heat until it wilts.

4. Turn off the heat, spoon in the Greek yogurt and add the paneer cheese. Mix everything together until all the ingredients are well combined and the cheese has melted a little. Take the Palak Paneer off the stove and serve while hot.

> **Recipe notes:**
>
> • *Paneer cheese can be found in Indian/Pakistani stores. If you can't get hold of it, substitute tofu or another solid, non-melting cheese such as halloumi.*

430 CALORIES **20g** PROTEIN **29g** FAT **20g** CARBS

MACROS (PER SERVING, EXCLUDING RICE)

SCOTCH EGGS

QUANTITIES BELOW
ARE FOR 1 SCOTCH EGG
(so you can easily adjust for
however many you make)

5 MINS PREP
25-30 MINS COOK

INGREDIENTS

1 egg

4 small chicken sausages
(total weight = 6oz/170g)

1 tablespoon dried polenta

METHOD

1. Preheat the oven to 180°C/350°F. Bring a saucepan of water to boil and, once bubbling, add in the egg. Set a timer for six minutes. As soon as the timer goes off, remove the egg from the pan and plunge it into a bowl of cold water.

2. Meanwhile, spread out a sheet of clingfilm on a chopping board and squeeze out the sausagemeat from the sausages. Spread thinly over the clingfilm with a spoon or using your hands.

3. Carefully peel the egg and place it on top of the flattened sausagemeat. Bunch up the clingfilm around the egg and, very carefully, massage the sausagemeat around it so that it is fully covered. Be careful not to break the egg while massaging the sausagemeat around it.

4. Pour the dried polenta into a bowl and add a good sprinkling of salt and pepper. Remove the clingfilm from around the Scotch egg and place it into the polenta. Roll the egg around gently, coating it completely.

5. Place the Scotch egg onto a baking tray and put it in the hot oven. For a soft yolk, leave in the oven for 20 minutes. For a hard yolk (better for keeping in the fridge for a couple of days to eat later), leave for up to 5 minutes longer (check that the sausagemeat is cooked fully before serving).

> **Recipe notes:**
> • If your sausagemeat won't stick together around the egg, mix in a teaspoon or two of beaten egg. If it is too sticky, add a little flour or protein powder.
> • You can use almost any kind of sausages for this recipe. Just don't try it with pork & apple sausages, as the apple pieces mean that the sausagemeat isn't sticky enough.

251 CALORIES

32g PROTEIN

10g FAT

10g CARBS

MACROS (PER SCOTCH EGG)

FRIED
CAULIFLOWER 'RICE'

SERVES 2

5-10 MINS PREP
10 MINS COOK

INGREDIENTS

2 rashers of turkey bacon

3 tablespoons/25g cashew nuts

1 teaspoon oil

½ teaspoon garlic, chopped

½ teaspoon ginger, chopped

a handful of spiralized or grated carrot

½ a cup of frozen peas

1 large egg

1 cup/100g cauliflower rice
(or ½ a small head of cauliflower
pulsed in a food processor)

1 tablespoon soy sauce

1 spring onion, chopped

METHOD

1. Heat up a large non-stick wok or frying pan
(no need to add in oil). Add in the turkey bacon
rashers and the cashew nuts. Be sure to keep moving
the cashews around so that they don't burn. After
around 3 minutes, turn over the turkey bacon rashers
and cook for another minute or two. When done,
remove both the turkey bacon and cashew nuts from
the pan and keep aside until needed.

2. Return the pan to the heat and add the oil.
When the oil is hot, add the ginger and garlic and
swirl around in the pan. When they have started to
become brown, but before they start to burn, add
the carrot and frozen peas and continue to stir.

3. Move everything to one side of the pan and crack
the egg into the empty space. Quickly stir it so
that the egg scrambles. Once it is scrambled, mix it
together with the rest of the ingredients in the pan,
stirring everything well.

4. Add in the cauliflower and mix everything
together. While the cauliflower is softening, add the
spring onion and, using some kitchen scissors, snip
the turkey bacon rashers into pieces over the pan.

5. Add the soy sauce, mix and serve immediately with
the cashew nuts sprinkled over the top.

> **Recipe notes:**
> • You can buy frozen ready-chopped ginger and
>   garlic, pre-spiralized carrot and cauliflower
>   rice and have this dish ready in 15 minutes
>   without any chopping.
> • In place of the turkey bacon, you can use regular
>   bacon or any leftover meat from your fridge.

 257 CALORIES **24g** PROTEIN **15g** FAT **16g** CARBS

MACROS (PER SERVING)

CRISPY CHILLI BEEF

SERVES 2

15 MINS PREP
10 MINS COOK

INGREDIENTS

½ pound/200g lean steak, fat removed and cut into strips (see Recipe notes)

2 tablespoons cornflour

2 tablespoons Chinese 5 spice powder

1 tablespoon oil

½ a red pepper, deseeded and sliced

½ a chilli pepper, deseeded and sliced

2 spring onions, sliced lengthwise

1 clove of garlic, chopped

small piece of ginger, chopped

1 tablespoon rice wine vinegar

1 tablespoon tomato ketchup

½ tablespoon soy sauce

> **Recipe notes:**
> • You can use any kind of steak for this recipe, but it's ideal for cheaper cuts such as Rump or Skirt steak. We are using the Chinese technique of velveting, which is almost a foolproof way of making meat tender and juicy. So save the expensive fillet steak for another recipe.

METHOD

1. Mix the steak strips together with the cornflour and Chinese 5 spice powder, making sure that they are well coated. Allow them to sit for around 10 minutes at room temperature, as bringing their temperature up will help them to get crispier.

2. Prepare the sauce – put the rice wine vinegar, tomato ketchup, soy sauce and a tablespoon of water in a jar, pop the lid on and shake vigorously.

3. Once everything is prepared, heat up the oil in a large wok or pan. Make sure it is really hot before adding anything.

4. Slowly add in the steak strips, making sure each strip has plenty of space. After 1 – 2 minutes, once they are starting to brown, turn them over and cook the other side. After this side is done, remove them from the pan.

5. Add all of the vegetables (except for the green parts of the spring onion) to the pan and stir-fry for approximately 3 minutes, making sure that the pan doesn't dry out by adding some water when necessary. Three minutes should be enough time for the vegetables to soften.

6. Turn down the heat, add the sauce and stir for a minute or two until it thickens.

7. Put the steak strips back in the pan and stir until they are well coated in the sauce.

8. Sprinkle the green parts of the onions on top before serving with rice and steamed broccoli.

250 CALORIES **25g** PROTEIN **9g** FAT **19g** CARBS

MACROS (PER SERVING, EXCLUDING RICE/BROCCOLI)

LOW CARB
COTTAGE PIE

SERVES 4

10 MINS PREP
30 MINS COOK

INGREDIENTS

2 teaspoons oil

1 large onion, chopped

1 medium sized carrot, chopped

1 stick of celery, chopped

¾ pound/300g lean mince

1 glass of red wine

1 beef stock cube

2 tablespoon tomato puree

a few dashes of Worcestershire sauce

a bay leaf (optional)

a couple of sprigs of thyme (optional)

a large cauliflower, pulsed in a
    food processor, or 3 cups/300g
    cauliflower rice

2 garlic cloves

2 tablespoons/25g butter

salt and pepper

½ cup/60g grated hard cheese such
    as cheddar

METHOD

THE BOLOGNESE SAUCE:

1. Heat up 1 teaspoon of the oil in a hot wok or frying pan and fry the onion until it begins to go soft and translucent. Add the carrot and celery and stir for a few more minutes (4 - 5 minutes should be enough).

2. Remove everything from the pan into a bowl. Add the remaining oil to the pan and heat it. Once the oil is very hot, add the mince.

3. Break up the mince with a fork while stirring, and cook until it has browned throughout.

4. Turn the heat down, add the red wine and crumble in the stock cube. Put the onions, carrot and celery back in the pan. Add the tomato puree, Worcestershire sauce, bay leaf and thyme.

5. Put the lid on the pan and simmer for around 10 minutes on low heat. Taste it at this point and adjust the seasoning if necessary (note: if there is too much liquid, drain it out or leave the lid off to evaporate some of it before moving on to the next steps as a watery Cottage Pie is not nice).

THE CAULIFLOWER MASH:

1. Peel the two cloves of garlic and put them into a pan with a lid, along with the cauliflower and a couple of tablespoons of water.

2. Cook the pan on medium heat for around 3 – 4 minutes, until the cauliflower is cooked.

3. Add in half of the cheese and all of the butter and stir gently until both have melted.

4. Season with salt and pepper and then fish out the two cloves of garlic.

THE COTTAGE PIE:

1. Take four mini casserole dishes and spoon the Bolognese equally into each of them. Top with the cauliflower mash and add the remainder of the cheese on top.

2. Cook in preheated oven at 180°C/350°F for around 10 minutes, until the cheese has melted. Remove the dishes from the oven and serve while hot.

324 CALORIES   27g PROTEIN   14g FAT   13g CARBS

MACROS (PER SERVING)

Recipe notes:

- These individual cottage pies freeze well. Take one out of the freezer in the morning and it will be ready to pop into the oven when you get home from work.
- The Bolognese sauce also makes a great low carb meal when served with courgetti and a good grating of cheese.
- The cauliflower mash is good accompaniment to any kind of meat in place of regular mash. Don't be tempted to leave out the garlic (and don't forget to fish it out at the end!).

FIRECRACKER CHICKEN

SERVES 3

15 MINS PREP
10 MINS COOK

INGREDIENTS

3 chicken breasts, chopped into
 bite-sized cubes

1 red chilli, chopped finely

2 – 3 cloves of garlic, chopped finely

1 tablespoon Sriracha

3 tablespoons brown sugar or sweetener

3 tablespoons soy sauce

2 tablespoons fish sauce

2 tablespoons tomato ketchup

1 tablespoon vinegar (rice or white wine)

1 tablespoon tamarind paste

1 teaspoon oil

1 onion, peeled and sliced

1 red pepper, deseeded and sliced

1 green pepper, deseeded and sliced

4 spring onions, chopped

a handful of sugar snap peas

1 pack of microwave rice

*Optional extras: 4 – 5 dried arbol chillies,
chilli flakes, black sesame seeds, a small
wedge of lime*

METHOD

1. Combine the chicken breast cubes with the red chilli, garlic, Sriracha, brown sugar or sweetener, soy sauce, fish sauce, tomato ketchup, vinegar and tamarind paste. Mix well and leave to marinate (for a minimum of 30 minutes but overnight if possible).

2. Heat up the oil in a wok or large frying pan. Before adding to the pan, drain as much of the marinade off of the chicken breasts as possible (the best way to do this is to fish them out carefully with a slotted spoon). Add the chicken to the hot oil and stir fry for around 3 minutes.

3. Add in the onion and stir fry for 2 - 3 minutes longer, until the onion begins to lose its stiffness.

4. At this point, add the peppers, sugar snap peas, the white part of the spring onions, the arbol chillies (if using) and the remainder of the marinade. Stir for around 5 minutes, until the sugar snap peas have softened a little.

5. Heat the rice up in the microwave according to the pack's instructions. Divide into 3 and spoon into a small bowl, pushing down with a spoon or with your fingers. Quickly turn the bowl over onto the centre of a large plate and give it a tap to release the rice. Sprinkle the chilli flakes, black sesame seeds and lime over the top (if using) and spoon the finished Firecracker Chicken around the rice.

480 CALORIES 54g PROTEIN 7g FAT 52g CARBS

MACROS (PER SERVING, INCLUDING RICE)

NEARLY
NO CARB BURGER

SERVES 2

10 MINS PREP
25 MINS COOK

INGREDIENTS

½ pound/250g lean steak mince

1 teaspoon ketchup or barbecue sauce

salt & pepper

1 teaspoon oil (for frying)

The bun:

2 eggs (yolks & whites separated)

a pinch of salt

2 tablespoons cream cheese

2 tablespoons/½ scoop of unflavoured
whey protein powder

1 tablespoon sesame seeds

METHOD

1. For the burger: mix together the mince, sauce and a good sprinkling of salt and pepper in a large bowl using your hands. Separate into two separate balls and flatten a little until they are in a burger shape.

2. Heat up the oil in a large frying pan and, once hot, add in the burgers. Fry on the first side for 2 – 3 minutes, until browned, then carefully flip over using a large spatula. Place a lid over the burgers and leave covered for approximately 8 minutes. Check that they are cooked thoroughly before serving – there should be no sign of any pinkness.

3. For the buns: add the salt to the egg whites and whisk until they are stiff and form peaks.

4. In a separate bowl, mix together the egg yolks, the cream cheese and whey protein powder until there are no lumps.

5. Carefully fold the egg yolk mixture into the egg whites, being careful not to flatten the egg whites too much.

6. Place a sheet of greaseproof paper onto a baking tray and spoon on the mixture to make four separate circles. Sprinkle sesame seeds on the top and put in a hot oven (180°C/350°F) for around 15 minutes, until the top of the circles have browned.

7. Remove from the oven and scrape the bun halves off the greaseproof paper as cleanly as you can using a metal spatula. Serve with the burgers and your choice of accompaniments.

338 CALORIES 38g PROTEIN 19g FAT 2g CARBS

MACROS (PER SERVING)

LOW FAT
CHICKEN TIKKA MASALA

SERVES 3

10 MINS PREP
25 MINS COOK

INGREDIENTS

2½ tablespoons of tikka spice mix

Juice of ½ a lemon

1 tablespoon oil

7oz/200g Greek yoghurt

2 chicken breasts, chopped into cubes

5 sprays of cooking oil spray

5 small shallots, chopped

3 cloves of garlic

1 tablespoon grated ginger

2 tablespoons tomato puree

½ a chicken stock cube

1 cup water

½ teaspoon brown sugar or sweetener

½ teaspoon garam masala

Recipe notes:
* *You don't have to grill the chicken (but I highly recommend that you do!). If you are short of time, you could skip steps 2 and 3 and simply add the chicken into the pan during step 5 to fry alongside the garlic, ginger and other ingredients.*

METHOD

1. First prepare the marinade: put 2 tablespoons of the tikka spice mix into a mixing bowl and add the lemon juice, oil and 3½oz/100g of Greek yoghurt. Mix everything together, add a good sprinkling of salt & pepper and throw in the chicken cubes. Mix it well so that the cubes are completely covered with the yoghurt and seasoning. Let the mixture marinate in the fridge for at least 30 minutes.

2. Take the chicken out of the fridge and thread onto bamboo skewers (tip: soak them in water for a few minutes first to stop them from burning).

3. Heat the grill to medium heat. Put the skewers on a grill pan and grill until they are cooked right through (this should take around 15 minutes). Turn over at least once during this time.

4. Meanwhile, heat up a frying pan or wok and spray in the cooking spray. Add the chopped shallots and cook for around 5 minutes, stirring frequently so that they don't burn (tip: you can add a few drops of water if they start to stick to the bottom of the pan).

5. Add the garlic, ginger, remaining ½ tablespoon of tikka spice mix, tomato puree and stock cube and stir them all together for around 1 minute.

6. Add the cup of water and allow the mixture to simmer until the shallots have become soft. Add more water if necessary, but the sauce should have a gravy consistency at this point, i.e. fairly thick.

7. Turn off the heat and add the remaining 3½oz/ 100g of Greek yoghurt, sugar/sweetener and garam masala, stirring the whole time. Unthread the chicken skewers from their sticks and add to the sauce. At this point, if the sauce is looking too thick, you can add a bit more water. Serve with rice or whatever else you choose.

MACROS (PER SERVING, EXCLUDING RICE)

Also by

LOUISE KANG, THE HIGH PROTEIN COOK

HIGH PROTEIN SWEET TREATS
100 HIGH PROTEIN BREAKFASTS

Go to http://classics/highproteincook.com
to download the electronic version of this book free of charge.